If I could see me now

Heather Garcia

BookLeaf Publishing

India | USA | UK

Presentation by *BookLeaf Publishing*

Web: www.bookleafpub.com

E-mail: info@bookleafpub.com

ISBN: 9788196218812

First edition 2022

DEDICATION

To my husband: Jeremi I love you always and forever. Thank you for always believing in me.

Zyla: for pushing me into walking out of the normal box I shoved myself into and letting me find me true self once again.

To every little girl, lost woman, to the ones who feel they don't belong, just know with brave wings we all learn to fly.

ACKNOWLEDGEMENT

To everyone that wants to follow their dreams,
go big! Never go small.

PREFACE

To the little girl,
To the girl behind every woman,
With brave wings,
We all learn to fly.

Prefect broken family

Man meet woman
They fall in love.
Well that's how the story usually goes.
Soon that love turns to hate,
Woman hates man.
That hate then gets projected to you,
You feel lost.
Alone.

Abandoned in this big crazy world.

Yet you're so small,
So innocent.
You play make believe inside your head,
Where mommy's and daddy's love,
And family always stay together.

But then you wake to your reality.
Broken glass on the floor.
You try to run and hide,
Try not to cry.
Tears fall as you scream.

Fist hits wall,
Fist hit skin,
Skin turns black and blue.
Is this love?
Mommy makes daddy leave,
Mommy let's daddy come home.
Don't say a word,
They alway say.
Let's pretend to be a perfect family,
No one needs to know your reality.

Man meets woman.
Well that's how my prefect broken story goes.

Self love trauma

They say you must love yourself before you love
another.
But what if you don't know how to love who
you are?

In today's world
We must look perfect.
Hair done, makeup on,the right clothes,
Let's not forget to be that perfect size.

In yesterday world,
Any woman was beautiful,
Especially her mind.

In reality we try to grasp perfection,
When in fact perfection is untamable.

When you try to be real and unapologetic,
Someone is there to crush those,
With the words that cut like a knife.

Self love is true trauma,
Because even when you look in the mirror,
You see every flaw,
Every scar.

Self love.
Self trauma.
Reaching for perfection,
When you're already prefect.

I am not Okay

I am not okay.

This bottle is getting too full,
Sometimes it is hard to keep the lid on.

The weight of my pain pushing me down,
But I smile.
I smile like it is all good,
That life is amazing.

When in fact the demons in my head,
They keep my reality in check.

God where are you?
Did you leave me to fight this battle?
Is this my test or this my last stand?

I am not okay.

But I cannot show that,
I must lie to myself so that others think,
I am okay.

That I want to scream,
Just to let my pain flow.

But then I remember,
I'm not supposed to not be not okay,
That I have great things in my life.

I am not okay.

But in this lifetime,
We are to be strong,
To not feel the bad but to feel the good,
You are weak if you show any kind of weakness,
That if you speak up that you are a snowflake,
But the pain that I feel is real.

Don't question God because he is in control,
But where is you God?

I have no scars or bruises to the eyes to see,
But the invisible scars that I do have show,
With each tear I silently cry.

I am NOT OKAY,
With a smile.

Broken

My heart is broken,
Yet it keeps beating,
Like heart that knows only love.

It sends blood to my organs,
Keeping my body moving.

But it'll never mend the brokenness inside.

I smile like tomorrow will come,
The sun always rises,
but we both know the night holds me hostage.

I just stare into the abyss,
Just hoping to feel the sun's heat on my skin,
to warm my cold soul from this hell.

Silent tears fall to the concrete below.
I hear the people outside this stone cold door I've
created.
The sting from knife burns my back.

Hard to trust.
Hard to hope.

It would be easy to stay here,
I've gotten use to being alone.
I am my own best friend.

For its me that hurts me.
Its never the doing of others.
I've laid my trust in them,
As they slowly turn me into the monster.

My heart is broken.

I'll keep going,
Like tomorrow is a new day.

For a parents love

Can't let you know just how you've hurt me.
The pain of waking up each day,
To never hearing "I love you".
To never feeling like I was good enough.

I'm in the in-between.

The tears they fall to empty hands.
My screams fall to empty ears.

Refusing to want more in life,
when I don't know what more ever was.

I see others with families,
Shower in love.

My heart is jaded.
This soul is torn.
I want it but I'm refused.

To know a mother's love.
A father's pride and joy.

I'm not the one fought after.

Cried over.
Loved.

I'm the joke
The failure.
The miss abortion that never was.
The wrong one.

My labyrinth,
This maze I've tried to outrun.

Trapped in my head.
Questions with no answers.
Answers with no questions.

Am I too broken?

Am I to far gone?

For a parents love.

Lost

The moon calls to me.
The stars are my bread crumbs.

I've always been lost this world.
That all call normal.
Never truly being who I felt I was.

Lost without a map.

Never allow to open my heart,
Open to a new world.

I find peace among the trees.
I found love within the rain.
I've dreamed in a field of lavender.
I prayed by the ocean.

The night is a long lost love.
Always calling you home.

The wind wrapping her arms around,
A chill brings a smile.

Maybe being lost is normal.

The boy

They started turning yellow.
Finally I don't have to keep covering them.

I must be careful and not say a word.

His lips crush into mine.
He loves me he says.
He wouldn't cause me harm.

It's my fault he does those things.

He only wants the best for me.

Isn't this what love is?

He slaps me.

What did I do?

I've dream of running away.
Finding myself among the innocent.
I'm not that strong.
He will find me.

I close my eyes.

I feel the sun on my face.

I turn around and I feel the arms,
Of the man who loves me.
As the nightmare of the boy,
Fades into the day.

My light

He is the only light in my dark.
He is truth I don't always hear.

He reminds me that I am good enough.
That he is to stay when the tough get hard.

He is who I lend on,
When the world turns on me.

He makes me laugh,
When all I want to do is cry.

Holds me.
Loves me.

He is is my light.

The unknown

Can you hear it?

Can you see it?

Can you feel it?

The moon calls to me.
To leave the the light of lies,
For the truth of night.

Would you change?

Would you stand your ground?

Would you believe?

The stars guide my path.
The wind shouts my name.
To be me is to leave me.

Travel into my unknown.

The little things

To dance among the flames.

To listen to rain hit the cold pavement.

To feel the first snowfall on my skin.

Watch the sun rise in the east and set in the west.

To hear the wind call to the moon

As if it was a spell of love.

Feel the sting of first love heartache,

To wonders of the soulmate.

Wish upon a shooting star.

The laughter of a babe.

Feel heartache of losing someone.

The little things be so big.

Broke

Broken in a million pieces,
Holding on the last string of rope,
Wondering is it time to let go?

When the tears no longer fall,
Sleep is an old friend that never calls,
Rather stay in the hole you've created.

Screaming in a room full of people,
For them to not even turn your way,
Its like you don't even exist anymore.

The rope starts to let go,
The last thread ready to give,
Breathe.

Would you be missed?
The world keeps revolving no matter what,
Would it matter any less or any more?

Scream once more,
Maybe they will hear now,
Broken.

When will it be

The smell of a newborn.
Softness of the skin.
The joy that feels your heart.

The negative test.
The tear stain pillow.
The heartache that haunts.

I feel as though I'm failing.
The one job I'm supposed to be able to do.
The fear of never holding my own.

The empty promises.
The unknown answers.
The unanswered questions.

The hurt I feel every time.
The pain behind my own smile.

When will it be my turn?
When will I have my glow?

Always

When I look into your eyes,
I see the world for its beauty.

When I feel your warmth,
It's like dancing on the sun.

When I feel your lips upon mine,
It's like kissing the clouds.

How your chose me?
I shall never understand.

You love me as though I'm the last.
You hold me as I might disappear.

When you hold my hand,
The world of yesterday disappears.

When you laugh,
It's like hearing choir of angels singing.

You may love me today,
I'll love you forever.

Always and forever.

Forever and ever…babe.

The witches

They say we will go to hell.
They say we don't really exist.
They say only in movies.

We say we do.
We say we are what you can't explain
We live among the stars and moon.

They say what we do is the devils work.
They say their God is the way.
They say their book is the rule.

We say we love all and respect all.
We say we can't harm.
We are what you fear.

They try to write us off.
Shine their light on us.

We live among the stars
For we are the witches of the night.

Life is hard

Life is hard.
Something we weren't taught.

Like how to love and how to survive.

Sink or swim
Never float.

We go through life just barely.
Forgetting the little joys.
But stressing on hard times.

We do we stop.
Smell the roses.
Feel the wind.
Touch the new grass.

Why must everything be so black and white?
When the grey is so grand?

What makes yesterday bad?
What makes today a present?
What makes tomorrow changeable?

Life is hard.

His Kiss

His fingers gently run down my back.
The chills of excitement.
He stops his lips above you
You reach out for the kiss,
He moves away.

You close your eyes,
Await the next move,
A smile runs across your face,
You feel his presence behind you.

He places his hands on your neck,
Runs his fingers up your head,
Grabs a handful of hair,
Pulls you back.

His lips crash on to yours,
Seconds turn to minutes,
Your breathe shortens.

He pulls away,
A smile upon his face,
He moves away.

You open your eyes,
Follow in his steps,
His love drives you insane,
As he throws you down on the bed.

One Day

One day this will all make sense.
The pain.
The heartache.

You may never understand,
Why you had to go through it all
What you could have done more?

One day you'll open your eyes,
Walk away from all that is bad,
Open your heart to all that's good.

You'll find that laughter is the best medicine

That rain brings rainbows.
The stars and moon are your friends.
The sun shines on the good.

It will make sense.
It will hurt.
But love will find it's way home.

Dear me

Dear me,
When the world fails you,
I love you.

Dear me,
It's not always as bad as it seems.
Remember the little things.

Dear me,
Yesterday is the past.
Today is the now.
Sleep tomorrow.

Dear me,
Always love with your whole heart.
Never allow hate to rule you.

Dear me,
Friends and family come and go.
But the real ones will always stay.

Dear me,
It's not your fault.
Just keep living.

www.ingramcontent.com/pod-product-compliance
Lightning Source LLC
La Vergne TN
LVHW010301200726
843506LV00014B/3338